Winter Day Poems:

For Sunny Day People

By Lennard Pierson

Published by Gray Hair Bandits Books

First U.S. edition, 2020
ISBN: 9798615391576

Printed in the United States of America

Dedication

Dedicated to my partner in life, Sharron Pierson,
and to my children and grandchildren.

Allow me to smooth my words,

Make them plain as paper,

On which I write words seeded

In soil both fallowed and frozen.

WINTER DAYS BLUES

WINTER TOO SOON

Clammy cold on naked skin

Chills the weakened soul.

Even the sun gives meager warmth.

Instead, thick air bites; the chill holds.

Babies cry. People moan.

We shiver under layered clothes.

Winter came too soon,

Surprised us all.

In cruel November, winter is too strong.

COLD AGAIN BUT WITH SUN

No wind. Only cold.

Flannel robes stay the chill;

Despite socks doubled, feet stay cold.

Every night: sleep deprived.

Yawns loud tell of nightmares.

Dry throats and dry coughs:

Are worse at sunset.

Take coffee black with honey.

Brisk walk in layered clothing,

Speaking of Budapest, Vienna and Prague:

Missing slick cobblestones; haunting old homes.

What is left after that? Memories forever fading.

WALK IN COLD

Bitter cold of yesterday now gone.

Icy morning. Warmer afternoon.

We bask in the sun; walk for blocks.

Enjoy now, we say, as we stride.

Tomorrow, deeper cold will knock.

Knowing this, we walk at slower pace

Inhale autumn air into our blood.

Today we are well; tomorrow we may freeze

BLUE BOAT

I am a boat much painted over:
Red, blue and yellow, stubbornly
Faded by winter's harsh tongue.
A leak in me, though plugged temporarily,
Allows cold waters inside in mournful drips.
Afloat I keep though stocked with fear
That one day I will sink to bottom.
Until now, I shadow this callous shore,
Hoping to keep that unkind day away.
Yet, I know that my cautious steering
Cannot keep me on course for long.
And I go about my aimless sailing,
Content in not having to go ashore.

IN EARLY MORNING THE BREEZE

Chills the old man's bones to the marrow,
Though for a time his flannel robe stayed the cold.
Now though his red robe is frayed and old,
Letting in icy air through tiny holes.

The clean, crisp air he draws his lungs burn,
Forcing him to shorten his breaths.
But soon, he knows, the sun will regain its throne,
Loosening the grip of winter on our souls.

On this day, the blue sky is free of clouds.
For a whisper of time, the cold does not sting.
Maybe today the old man will smile,
Darkness rising from his repentant soul
And be as light as a breeze at noon.

PRISONERS OF AGE

In the afternoon the sun at last awakes.
Windows caked with weeks-old dust
From an unpaved church parking lot
Let in sunlight too shy to sit down and visit.

Yesterday, weeping clouds had hidden the sun,
Filling the house with light that fades like dust.
Good news for those slow of foot:
For winter sun is harsh on skin that hides indoors.

In the houses of prisoners of old age
Thick and heavy drapes keep sunlight out.
Hushed fear chains them to their cold beds.
Old feet no longer feel true ground.

Even so, life after death does not hold them close.
Content are they with the freedom
Their chains gift to them.

ANGRY WINTER RAIN

Hard, cold rain like heaven's arrows fell after dark,
Northwest storms arriving as forecast
By low, bruised clouds over thirsty ground,

Surprising us under winter covers,
Startling those wrestling with sleep
Tiptoeing through the house on pillow feet.

Thunder made the walls shudder;
Made the dining room chandelier sway long:
Like a bomb blowing walls down.

That night the wind blew shingles off roofs;
Blew down an old elm tree, crushing
A red truck parked on a dark street.

The howling wind made us sit up,
Eyebrows wrinkled, ears perked up to listen

For blind objects striking the house.

Two houses down lightning struck;

Seconds later our lights went dark

Hail pelting mournful windows,

Dirty from last summer's dust.

Fear flowed throughout the house;

Frightening darkness filled our minds,

As we fear our shelter has not kept us safe;

For what we humans build,

Nature can quickly break.

With morning light, we gaped at the broken homes

Of those who prayed be spared from loss.

That day we learned that storms come and go,

Indifferent to passionate prayers to God alone.

COLD MOURNING COFFEE

Mornings I brew coffee in my kingly red robe,
Pacing later a room with windows many,
Like someone that speaks only in his head.

Staring at the sky that wants to cry over a death,
On creaking knees, I pray for God, our sun,
To come again to give me new hope

That this deep sorrow burrowed in my soul
Will end when the ice on the lake breaks
And the sun takes off its heavy coat.

I leave a cold window to help my spouse
Prepare for a job that hollows her soul
And when the stars are brightest leave her drained

On the green couch used to pray for sleep.
When she opens the door to the cold air,

Her face white as the snow piled outside,
I feel as if I walk alone, feet bare, on an icy lake.

After the door is closed and warmth returns,
I stand at the bay window, robed in red,
Unable to compose my day or work

Like when I could axe wood for winter
And feed my floundering dream
Of leaving tracks deep in whitest snow.

DEATH IN WINTER

We do not think of death until a loved one dies.

When such death happens, we measure our coffin size,

See in mind's eye mourners sprinkling us with eternal dirt,

While others hold handkerchiefs to teared up eyes,

Giving hearty thanks to God to be alive

And having not to leave too soon this life,

Spending eternity on heavenly dunes.

Though thoughts of death do soon dissolve,

As memories of dead loved ones fill up our minds.

NEW YEAR'S DAY AGAIN

Another year of the Gregorian calendar has passed
Into our sacred human history good and bad.
Ahead are events that may cut like daggers.

Our pain may bleed and pool at our feet,
Our dreams grow old from over use.
Fresh dreams, not watered, will die from thirst.

A drought of many lives will strike our crops,
Dashing our hope for a winter with warmer nights.
We will see more fire and ice, more loss of life,

And winds strong seek to crush our spirit.
But come the last days of the old year,
We will forget our misfortunes and hail

The promise of another new year.
It is what we humans can do
When our times are but a sea of troubles.

ALL DAY COLD

The rain was cold and fell like bullets,
Icy and thick, stinging on skin uncovered,
Holding us back from walking outdoors,
Making us sullen prisoners of the trapped air.

We wore our flannel red robes all day,
King and queen in our drafty house,
Believing hail and snow would fall,
As it often falls on our too troubled land.

Unlike our embattled neighbors north,
Neither ice nor snow fell on us.
The darkened somber day console did not,
Giving us no cheer to warm our hearts.

Enclosed in a closet room, dimly lit, peasant-like,
Our bodies wanted more distance between us all,
For much closeness made us speak strong words,

No sooner said—regretted.

Though our eyes did not smile,

Or our mouths spoke soothing words,

We were content to share same space,

To be safe from the storm that kept us afraid.

CHRISTMAS EVE

We celebrate Christmas Eve us two alone,
Observing this day with our thoughts gone far,
Our eyes staring, staring at a flat square screen,
Our small artificial Christmas tree lights blinking,
Blinking as if drained by forced cheers and laughs.
We raise neither glass nor cheer to life beyond,
Content to savor this life though short and mean,
Fueled by failures and sorrows that sting.
The cold night is as if from foreign land.
Outdoors, a hungry black dog without home barks
At shadows that haunt the shivering night.
On a faraway tree, a huge owl proclaims:
Our shortest day has so soon passed.
Winter's icy hands will take firm hold tomorrow.
Tonight, we gaze into each other's eyes
And drink to our childhood sorrows.

MEMORIES THAT BREATHE

AUTUMN BIRTHDAYS

A September cold day of birthday celebrations,

In which summer has long expired,

And fall's inspired breath blows leaves off shivering trees.

Velvet cake we eat along with creamed coffee.

Our birthday song breaks down; we laugh embarrassed.

We talk about a brother two years dead.

Sad clouds hover over our deaf and dumb table.

Tears dried, we give thanks for life,

Though it too, we know, will be short and light.

DAUGHTER'S BIRTHDAY

Despite dark clouds at war above,
His daughter's birthday brings smiles
To the father's face, engraved by long winters
And summers that darken his spotted face.

He tells her to honor this special day,
Placing high this unique space shared by them,
Ignoring the dreariness spreading across the land;
Seeing the face of splendid spring
In the angry storms that winter brings.

PUT A PIN IN HER HEART

Put a pin in her heart, she that at night
Kisses me lips to lips
And walks away softly
In a dream that blooms before sunrise,
Releasing me from the coming of light,
Ending when my feet feel the cold ground;
A sweet memory savored slowly
More than one hundred times.

Such thoughts that sleep walk come to me,
Even now when I read of a gypsy woman
Walking on a cold Irish beach,
This temptress of the sultry night
Who walks in my restless mind.
More than once I shout, "Turn away!"
For I have made deep footprints on this path,
On which losing one's bearings bears awful pain
That knows of hearts broken and bleeding

And how it feels for new blood to turn old.

Wary of the thorns of the past

Piercing my skin fragile now,

Tearing like paper, leaving raw scars.

And I turn away desire and bury my eyes

In books, pages musty and yellowed,

Free to live off dust covered memories

Fading with each passing year.

A GARDEN OF HEAVEN

As an icy north wind moved in,

Gathering clouds into enormous balls,

We donned surgical masks

To keep from breathing

Spring air bad for our task.

Despite the smell of rain

Heavy in the dark clouds soaring above

We dug our hands into brown soil,

And planted quickly, glancing up

At the churning sky glaring down at us,

Lightning tearing through the massive clouds,

And the humid air cooling as the storm approached.

Afraid, I warned my wife and ducked inside.

But wanting to complete the task she stayed

On knees much swollen from digging,

Not yet recovered from a frightening cold,

Yet resolute she to work more minutes outdoors,

Where she relives her childhood on a dairy farm,
Playing outside in the ditches near the fence,
With her two sisters playing until sunlight dimmed,
When their mother called to them from the barn.

While I inside think that when I'm gone,
More certain now than yesterday,
She will solace find in her garden dirt,
And move away from my ashes planted in air.

This thought brings to my dry eyes a smile:
Our garden will hold us together even after I die.

BIRTHDAY

We sat at a booth by a window frosted over,
Celebrating the February cold in which she
Was born, forcing me to see her with fresh eyes
That let her in whole.
Listened I to her intently, shutting out
The other's chatter and titters.

Hands on table, with both ears I listened.
This was her hallowed hour,
To speak at length of her farm days;
Of father and mother milking cows
In a round barn much too cold,

Fingers icy as water in their freezing pond.
She's a sweet, angelic woman
Deserving more than me,
For I'm prisoner of thoughts dark that wander far
In a mind like desert dust crossing waters wide.

MOTHER'S DEATH REMEMBERED

Two autumns gone.

Pain still raw.

November Ninth, ordinary day

Made extraordinary by a mother's death.

Death witnessed by two sons and a daughter.

Helpless, they look on as their mother's heart stops.

Tears plenty, their hearts beat wild.

She lies buried steps from her husband's,

Long dead, low-born grave.

Both parents now gone,

The brothers and the sister

Feel a deep-well loss; confused their thoughts,

They face uncertain a future motherless and afraid.

REGRETS THAT NEVER REST

A FOOL'S OBSESSION

He thinks again of the woman
Whom he has not seen exposed,
Knowing nothing true about her,
Guessing only from experience
That she has feelings for him,
Showing this with her eyes and hands.

Knowing of his weakness, long-suffering,
He wishes he's wrong; wants to be wrong.
Yet, her blue eyes and how she styles her hair
Makes his blood flash through like a current.
Something about how she speaks speeds his heart.
He wants her, but he also wonders why.

They are not a good match—he believes this fully.
And, yet, he still wants her truly, though desire
Makes him shake his head in blind disbelief.
He does not want to imagine her aging breasts,
Nor her wrinkled neck or spotted hands.
But cannot explain the way he feels when around her.

His eyes go to her whenever she's near

And he so wants to kiss her delicate lips.

This an obsession even Heaven cannot explain.

Desire is seen when desire is blind.

The man cannot put her lips, her eyes and voice

Out of his bromidic mind.

Obsession, he cries, should die a quick

And welcome closing of its eyes.

SPENT STORM

My self-made storm has fizzled.

Yet, storm subdued, I still say words that hurt;

Words that sting even in air I breathe.

My malicious storm has beat

The ramparts until spent.

My rough seas tamed truly.

Though the awful damage to the shore is real.

And I well know now that

What's broken will never sufficiently heal.

TIME OF REGRET

Drizzling morning, leaves splayed
On a wet deck of a humble home near a lake.
Blustery winds blow dried leaves off trees
Into small piles that soon make
Their way to a chain-link fence.
At noon slate-gray rain clouds block the sun,

And low fog curls around the barks of trees,
Spurring him to think of time lost,
How time is short; death long.
He yearns for days of mugs raised
To health and friends now done,
Recalling old cheers, spirited laughter,

And when women spoke of food and men,
Singing rowdy songs mocking them.
Such times his tongue loosened, feet danced,
Lips kissed maidens, cursed by them,
Called fresh and rude; rightly so.
At home a young wife awaits,
Half afraid of another long cold night alone.

A DISASTER THAT BINDS

The cold clouds swamped the broken day,

Shrouding us in their enduring lament.

Soon the bully breeze stung our eyes,

Making us cough to clear lungs grown weak:

Forcing us to rub our eyes and weep

Silently in the busy street

Over the disaster that now binds us all

Like tribes of old scattered far,

Or slaves in chains in ancient times.

A disaster we saw approaching

With the coming of clouds swift and cold,

For which we must now endure eternal pain foretold.

AT THE HAIR SALON

At the hair stylist, a gray-haired man,
His youth long passed its prime,
Stares blankly at his phone as he waits
For the stylist with friendly ears.

While outside the sky sprinkles cold rain
On the unsuspecting hair of walkers.
Dark, cold storm clouds above over all roll,
Threatening to smash ice balls on us when we sleep.

But, for now, I too wait for the young, female hair artiste,
Who, unmarried with child, desires to become a nurse.
I ask her about herself, preferring to speak not of me.
But I do tell her about selling our house, moving away

From a neighborhood we no longer can afford.
We talk as friends of many years, speak quietly.
She listens, is kind and soft-spoken, good at cutting hair.
My hair now cut, I'm saying goodbye,
For there will be not a next time;
When one is ill, tomorrow is not a promise sealed.

BLACK DOG

A black dog behind a wood fence barks
Now and before now as well,
Barks like a puppy, wagging its tail,
Without a mother to put down its fear.

Fear of strangers, fear of other dogs, fear of the dark,
Left alone in a square, grassless space with stones,
From where it cannot escape or find freedom
In the muddy alley behind its owner's home.

My "black dog" is like that dog,
Which comes to me at dawn,
When I stare out a window,
I feel such a heaviness embrace me,

Unable to find calm or peace
In a troubled, tortured mind,
A prisoner of my sinful deeds,
Unwilling to open the door to leave.

NO FINAL ENDINGS

UNFINISHED CHORE

Clouds and wind spin like dancers in a blue field.

A pushy cold wind wants to blow me down.

I fight it off like a leaning tower.

With shoulder that hurts I sand the deck,

Inhaling dust that my weakened lungs burn.

The still air feels like it has showered.

From far away I smell a deep earthly rain,

Subtle warning of an icy downpour soon.

Today, though, it is but a faithless warning.

Rain does not fall this day, not here not now.

The wind bends branches, blows off leaves,

Forcing me to leave my final chore at ease.

AWAY FROM DEATH

Before now he spoke of death with smile ironic,
Though wishing not to welcome death too soon,
Taking care of body and soul to live more years
Than a long buried forgotten father.

That he not need fake teeth to eat or smile.
That he makes his goal before old age cuts him down.
But then mother and brother die six months apart.
Time to speak of approaching death had come.

Where once time was long to listen to words around,
To sit and watch worried none by his final exit ahead,
Seemingly at greater distance from here,
With more careful look, he now sees death with him.

WALK IN FAITH

Clouds high, wide like long rivers

Do not hide an angry sun,

For on this day no rain falls

On a thirsty land of deepening cracks,

Where no welcome wind blows,

Leaves wilt, shadows shrink;

Afternoon air pauses to rest.

Or later churns and kisses ground.

Despite fear, we walk a path

Shared by other feet, staring long

At houses stripped by scorching heat,

Eyes on a somber sky, we walk in faith,

Daring old gods to do us no more harm.

MISTED EYES

Cold, bully rain punches from three sides.

Wind blows southeast long ways.

On park bench below an ancient tree,

We sit and see long into the tall grass,

Our eyes misted by long rain.

Under a tall oak, flush with leaves,

We eye hard rain pelting dirty windows.

In this small space we live safe,

Though so near we taste renewed rain

From far ocean beyond frozen peaks.

We in another land, one we dream of,

Await storm's end to restart our journey,

A trek so far twelve troubled years long

On this same deeply rutted road of ours.

A WAITING ROOM

In a brightly lit waiting room, talk
Is of a refrigerator broken down;
A woman fusses on her phone
About where to buy a new fridge;

A seventy-three-year-old black woman
Laments to a white man of black men
Who grow up without a dad at home.
The white man leans forward, perks

His ears to show he cares,
Though he has cancer in his kidneys
And death sits with him everywhere.
The black woman, a former public-school teacher,

Speaks her truths voice confident, fair,
Enough to be heard above TV noises polluting the air.
The TV news reader speaks of snow and storms,
And of a South American dictator who has died.

Meanwhile, I read my book, trying to stay

In my own private space, alone,

Keeping above the fray, thinking

Nothing new under the sun today.

SADNESS THAT BLEEDS

If I love tomorrow as today,

I will feel big sadness that bleeds,

Fed by pain and loss most deep.

To keep the black dog at bay,

Set obsession's flaws free,

And turn away forever from

A maze of hurt that made me a slave.

ROAD TO HEAVEN

The road to heaven
Does not go through here:
A hard land of spiny weeds,
Of rocks scattered far afield.

At our house of stone, salvation does not
Take a chair at our broken table.
Here we whisper, throats dry as desert sand.
Eyes we keep on ground long cracked by thirst,

Knowing we can do our worst
In a broken land like ours,
Where our gods do not live.
And our lives become drained of worth.

SURPRISE RAIN

It poured like a huge barrow of rain
Dumped on our homes asleep,
Cascading over gutters filled with wrinkled leaves,
Overwhelming their spirits long spent.

Rain waterfalled down a torn umbrella sleeve
Onto the deep-cracked concrete patio floor,
Taking us all by surprise,
As rain had not been foreseen.

But fall it did, a half hour, cooling
The hot air that until then enslaved us.
At the sliding glass door, we stood alarmed,
Feeling a chill run down our spines.

Awed by the fury of nature,
And its indifference frightening.
When the rain ended, our silence resumed,
Humbled again by what we cannot presume.

FACE OF TRUTH

Eyes pop open to monster rain clouds

Hovering on the other side of our glass door.

From a fragile safety of our home we glare,

Our mouths open, dazed by the fury of a storm,

Dreading angry gusts will peel off the roof.

Greatly fooled, we are awestruck:

It pours; hail knocks hard.

Lightning strikes a pole; we go dark.

Our oasis exposed to ice

As lightning strikes dazzle,

Frightening us in darkness' lumpy cloak.

Unable to blind our eyes or silence thunder's growl,

On aching knees we pray God indeed is on our side.

BLUE RELATIONSHIPS

BOY WITH MATCHES

The kid with matches plays,
Sets the dresser curtain ablaze,
Landing the child in bad boy jail

Made of concrete: home of big dogs;
Here he spends one soul-crushing day,
Shedding tears hot with shame,

Learning quickly to hate
His jailer, a drunken father,
Filled with buried pain.

ON THE BLACKTOP ROOF

At night the asphalt roof cooled enough,

Freeing it from a fierce daytime sun.

There the boy scored the southern stars

In a deep black sky of pulsating lights.

Because of the girl, he climbed on that roof

Obsessed to catch a glimpse of her

Through lighted gaps in mango trees.

His hardened passion moved his stars,

Routing him onto a path uneven, strewn with stones.

That day guided him into a corner to be alone.

And when he left for a year, he thought only of her,

A girl too young, confused by attention and love.

For she was an invention in his mind blinded by lust.

Despite warnings from his mother,

He married her though not in church.

Years later, children older, he took his leave.

MEMORY OF A KISS

Torrential rain reminds me always
Of the rainy evening I saw her cross the street,
Her beloved returned holding a large umbrella

Above her long, dark curled hair I loved.
Saw her skip from curb to rain-covered street,
Shimmering on pooling water lights,

Falling raindrops framed in a fogged streetlight.
With each step, she of high cheekbones and eyes deep,
Left forever my liar's life in rubble.

Depart she did for that island where she was born,
To grow old with her man while I have grown old alone.
Standing here, by this sliding glass door, I feel a death chill.

And a cruel sadness chokes my breath.
So much to regret: Things not done or said.

For a short time, she and I were secret lovers,

If only in our minds; and only while keeping

My sinful secret hidden far from her.

Thus, I who sought love so desperately drowned in its loss.

MONDAY MORNING STACKS

On Monday morning a library glows
With the high-pitch voices of children
Too young to be in wealthy private schools,
Brought here by mothers who do not work.

In the rear of the library, next to the book stacks,
Sit an elderly couple reading: she about Budapest;
He about listening fairly to the other side.
But he also looks up to listen to a boy who says

"No!" to his gentle, young, harried mother.
The elderly woman is white, her husband brown.
They speak with soft voices, whispering almost.
From time to time, he stands and walks.

Unlike other old men here, he strolls,
Shoulders pinned back, chest raised.
Other times, he sniffs cool air, stares at women
In the well-lighted library stacked with great books.

He also writes in a brown slender copybook.

His eyelids close; soon he's dozing, arms crossed.

He's another of the men that use libraries to pass the time,

Whose adulthood dream is shelved like many a dusty book.

DUTY BOUND

Up early: dress, drink coffee and clean shave.

Drive miles north to breakfast with a grandson.

Grandparent duty, last of this year, thank god.

We are expected to show up, wave the flag.

Hooked us with bacon, eggs and pancakes.

The grandson cleans the plate; wants more.

He has a big stomach, he says, still eating.

But it's time to go; the line is out the door.

Drink up. Leave. The young are waiting.

It went well, wasn't all that bad.

Could have worn a more tattered coat.

You could have been writing sad stories.

Instead, on this day you're a dutiful grandparent.

Hurrah!

FATE'S CUFFS ON ME

I sit—radio speaking of police brutality—
And place a feverish, spotted hand
On my aching head: of this world I despair.
This broken world much like a bloodied wheel.

Cold rain fell today before dark,
As more intense ache grips me still.
I blame the wandering wind traveling east.
On aging feet, my world sways,

Grounded once now unhinged.
Fate has placed its cruel cuffs on me.
If not for it, what more could I be?
No answer found in a grieving mind,
Only the loss of unbridled dreams.

SLEEPLESS

I drove at slow speed, thank God.

It was late, daylight waning.

Without warning, my eyes closed.

When I opened them again, I saw tops of trees,

As if I were lying in a field staring at the sky.

Awake now, fear surged through my brain.

Clearly, I had fallen asleep while driving.

My God! In busy traffic too.

Alas, I had not yet crashed.

But I was lost, unsure of my whereabouts.

Something came over me, told me to turn around,

Which I did, heart in hand.

I found my way; gave thanks to God

And His warning this time I took to heart.

A MAN AND A WOMAN

A man and a woman in dark clothes,

Their hair grey and softly limp,

Sit on a bench at a Hungarian church.

Light rain falls on their wrinkled hats.

Snuggled like new lovers, they don't seem to mind

The cool air sprinkled with raindrops,

Falling like snow melting in spring.

Their liver-spotted, calloused hands touch,

Having endured the cruel Soviet iron rule.

Those days of empty stomachs they do not forget,

Though they were most alive then.

Now, during a winter evening,

They sit and wait, rarely smile.

In the new world, they are totally lost.

A LADY'S CONTENTMENT

She reads in her office on a couch,

The radiator heater turned low,

As moist air cools the room.

She seems content, smiles at life.

This despite unwise words,

That makes her heart bleed alone.

But tomorrow the sun will stand,

Hope and heart strong,

And she will leave to spend a day

With children she loves more than life.

Leaving her cross at home: a foolish man.

She willingly puts down his questionable love,

Sets it aside, lets it turn blue, lets it die on a vine.

For what matters most in life is her happiness,

Driven by a love of freedom and a hint of deepest hope.

NIGHT TAKES A WALK

Night puts on its black heavy coat,

Walks down cobblestoned streets,

Around the block it smokes a pipe.

Hears two cats in heat, a baby cry,

And men's drunken laughter ring out of a fog,

Cheap Austrian wine warms their potbellies.

The evening is smooth; meat cooked smells divine.

Working people have settled down.

Some have eaten dinner and gone to bed.

Others sit entranced before a cold TV screen.

Not Night: it will be hours before it can sleep.

Only reluctant dawn can stand down.

Still in bed dawn and under covers warm.

THE SINKING SUN

Was in good spirit as we left this land
Of grass tall as man, of cattle wearing thick coats
For another land farther south, across two wide rivers,
Where the ground is fertile and fresh.

Straight as a ribbon, the black top road stretches far,
Never ending, it seems to our tired, wary eyes.
When the sun sinks below the tallest trees,
But the night's tired eyes are not yet open,

Our hearts beat faster wanting to get to the big city
Of many glass buildings tall and cold,
Before our eyes see no longer the narrow road.
Sunlight gone, the stars closer seen.

But on the road darkness but a heavy cloud
That kisses ground and unravels our animal fears.
In such open spaces where no houses live
Both people and cattle are not safe from bad spirits,

Walking about the land after the sky has gone to sleep.

During this silent time, we dare not speak a hopeful word.

Neither do we open ears to frightening cries at night.

But pray that we will soon be saved by big city lights.

WOMAN ON A FARM

The old woman who lives alone on a farm
Tells stories from the heart rooted in her past
Covering more than nine decades long.
She and her dairy farmer husband
Milked cows on days their pond froze
And the milk barn filled with icy air,

Their breaths condensed to frost.
While raising three children, they fought to find rest
Whenever they could place a firm hand on it.
With many chores to complete, the hours had long reach.
Then time came on quick feet and spoke truth to them.
Her man's mind would soon not be his anymore.

He would fall; he would see things not there.
She saw him die and buried.
Alone now, she makes her way while waiting
For her time to die in a favorite chair.

But death arrives not on the swiftest feet,

For patient death does not rush anywhere.

It has nowhere to go, no chores to undertake.

Her fate: to wait and wait in her favorite chair.

SOLO MAN

COLD MAN AMONG THE STACKS

People do not look up
Even to see if you are a man
Standing on corners begging
For bread or wine;

Or an old man with walker,
Dragging feet toward the stacks.
To them you do not matter.
You have come out of the cold,

Icy air comes in behind you.
You walk to where thick books fill the room,
Seeking space far from eyes that glare.
Today, you are ashamed of you:

A man who speaks true words that hurt.
A man who sees the forest not the trees,
A man who has wronged too many times,
Sinned in mind and body, lusted wrong.

But wishes only to hurt no more,

Lift the burden off shoulders now grown weak.

Not to an aging, indifferent God kneel

But to man forgiveness plead.

HEARTBROKEN

I'm sitting in the rain in a wooded park,
Long and narrow with many shade trees,
Under which excited young lovers meet
After the sun, angry all day, takes its leave.

On this rainy day the breeze blows cold;
Far-traveled dark clouds weep
Even in a steady rain, fine as mist,
I don't seem to mind it soaking my clothing.

All this time I've been crying,
Feeling cold and sorry for myself.
A girl I love does not love me.
I had no courage to tell her how I felt.

Long years have travelled far on foot.
Now lost in an uneven fog—her name.
Her long, dark, curled hair shapes her face.
Her eyes are large, her mouth small.

Older than me—she—I truly believe.

But I think only of her as if I need her to breathe,

Which I know no longer is true.

It rains as if the sky were shedding my tears.

I seem to rejoice in my self-inflicted pain,

Born from a young life that grew old too soon.

A VERY UNLUCKY MAN

He sits in a wheelchair in a one-room house,

A large man weighing much more than he should,

His right leg sawed off at the knee,

After slipping on a wet airport floor.

Trapped in a wheelchair he despairs,

Chronic asthma racking his already tortured lungs,

A river of steroids weakening his aging bones.

Despite his cross, endured with resentful resignation,

He did not give up on life.

It gave up on him.

NIGHTMARE IN WINTER

I'm in an underground shelter with many seats,
Waiting like others for something to happen,
Looking around like birds watching out for a hawk,
Ready to dart to the safety of sleeping trees.
A shoebox and a briefcase are all I have with me
Knowing not why these two things.
Confused, I look around as if I don't belong.
We seem to be sheltering from something I can't see.
No one speaks or shares.
A storm, perhaps?
My mind speeds but stuck on what to do,
I think only of saving myself somehow.
At last, I walk up a long staircase to ground level.
Horrified, I see water from the sea reaching the stairs.
I panic and rush downstairs, holding on to a cold rail.
Grabbing my things, I sprint upstairs,
Two stairs at one time.
Head north, I say, away from the flood.
It's common sense: choose life—run!
Which I do, leaving others to drown.

MAN ZERO

Where the house once stood red dirt remains.
Leveled to its foundation, no trace of life left.
Now the street but a mouth with a missing tooth,
A wide, ugly hole cruelly exposed.

Big truck mud tracks streak the street
Despite the wild, howling cold rain
That did not wash these tracks away.
In that house an old black man lived alone,

Sitting often on the porch in the dark.
In silence, he watched young walkers
Speaking of the weather or of good times.
Some evenings he grilled on the porch,

Drank beer with a man who glared at us.
But one day we no longer saw him on his porch.
He might have died, we presumed.
Or gone to an old folks' home;

Gone as if he had never lived a minute here.
Missed by none: another forgotten grave.
A fate long to be dreamed and wished for.

STANDING GUARD

You feel crushed inside by words barbed,

Breaking skin, oozing bad blood;

You are dispirited by the bite of words

Not weighed by clear reason.

But you are not made of sweet milk;

Your heart is hard; your anger a well.

Love you sweep away with wiry broom,

Standing guard at your border post aloof,

Where no one crosses without careful look.

Even your smile hides a contempt for others:

Those who believe you to be good;

Those who hate you with good reason.

Only God knows what is true in you

And can forgive the hard heart of a fool.

ON A FEARFUL ROAD

LAST ROAD TRIP

It was to be our last long road trip,
Last drive west to Montana,
To the mountains far from us,
Escaping the Texas heat that kills,
Saying time is drying out.
Illness doesn't sun on beaches.
While each day we creep closer to cremation.

We drove three days until the sky's light dimmed,
Taking in wind turbines, barbed wire,
Over flat land vast and empty,
On which cattle huddled swapping away flies
Harassing them until night drives them away.
On this our last road trip, storms overtook us:
Strong winds, rain and pea-size hail fell,

Forcing us to shelter under trees tall and strong,
To wait out the front-range storms,
Holding us back from reaching our room
Until the sun dying passes over to the other side.

Despite sore backs and weakened wills,
The next day we're back on our journey,
Knowing that we must go on,

Must go on to confront the lonely road
Before darkness whole cuts short
Our last long road trip together.

FEAR IN THE DARK

When the sun is done and unnatural light shrinks shadows,
We retreat to our cold homes, closing our dusty blinds,
And fading into the walls of our framed stick houses.

As animals do when they take shelter in their shells,
We withdraw into the brittle safety behind walls.
For beyond the porch lights the night obscures.

We keep our distance from creatures out there
Luring us into the cold arms of patient darkness,
Hoping to save ourselves and our timid life.

BUDAPEST IN AUTUMN

Our apartment on the second floor
At which we arrive sleepy and dazed
After a long ride in the night sky,
On feet long cooped in shoes,
Is too warm an evening in late October
In old Budapest of secrets buried,
Making it hard to gain good sleep.

Morning arrives on sluggish feet,
Our bodies beaten by meager sleep.
We eat bread and sausage, drink black coffee;
And later cross three bridges over the Danube,
Our eyes filling up with a panorama of old buildings,
And an ancient river isolating hills from flat land.
For a day we are young again, our travails forgotten.

LOST IN A DESERT OF FEAR

A few hours from where we drove

The road narrows, brush roughs us

Along the road flat, long, alone;

Above us the proud sun stings;

Below we feel our lungs inhale

Hot air, desert air, from the west country

That with night cold rolls in,

Sucking up a body's warmth.

Weariness took us by the scruff of neck,

Shaking us as if we were mere pups,

Feeding us fear that we would not reach our home,

Be trapped in our vehicle in dry brush country,

Prisoners to cries and sounds in the December night,

Huddled together for body warmth,

Listening to hungry animals wanting to eat.

Trembling, we prayed and waited for daylight.

When it came, we stretched our slender arms,

Stood on the long road, took in growing warmth,

Storing our bloated fears back into our heads
And sat cross-legged on the harder ground
Until we felt strong enough to go on.

SEPARATION

A throat sore and offended awakens me at dawn,
Under freshly washed white cotton sheets,
During a rainstorm that makes gutters sing
And pounds the wood deck with cold rain.

My partner sleeps soundly next to me,
Breathing smooth, at ease,
Tonight, she does not moan,
Her sleep freed from persistent pain.

In an hour the alarm will ring strong,
Better rise now than to think long
About my flight later today,
Leaving her alone a fortnight.

Miss each other, of course, we will:
Separations wear us to ground,
Loads our hearts as if with lead.
Leaving us speaking to ourselves.

But go I must, say goodbye with a kiss
And fly to the land of deep spring snow
To take a break from her chemotherapy
And from my own imminent death.

URGENT SURGERY

We hear the clarion call of urgent surgery,
Of a man known to us as a world traveler,
One that endures pain, takes small steps,
Leaves faint footprints in mud hardened.

True, mortality whispers urgently in our ears,
Warning words that we must heed,
Though we are nevertheless shocked
When it taps our shoulders humbled.

Mortality is fleshed thickly in my head
When a surgeon's scalpel cuts deeply
Into searing doubts, fumbling fears,
Drawing blood thinly shed in a cup.

Talk now of decisions already marked,
Second-guessed, likely made in haste.
By now time is but a drop of water,

Lingering not long on thirsty ground.

When his eyes close on the operating table,

His short sleep is life or death enabled.

UNPAID SINS

We know ourselves best when memory
Makes us slaves of past harms made,
And when it tears at our insides unawares,
Though the wound bleeds, we do not blame ourselves.

Memories of women that would not or should not forgive,
Behaviors ugly as twisted branches in rampant weeds,
Grown taller by a torrent of long-suffering shame
That taint the good done in a weed-free life.

Dark sins dust covered that do not blow away
Even when a strong wind exposes these to brightest light.
Grim are these tortured sins cursed by deepest remorse.
A life well lived does not wave off forgotten sins,

Nor does knowledge of one's raw self free one
From the shackles of imprisoned guilt.
Longing to breathe fresh air,
We bend our knees, kissing cold ground,

Raise our wrinkled hands to God,

Groan our sorrow deep in our bellies,

Unable to let our darkest grief out.

WINTER ABIDES IN ME

In my brain winter storms don't end,
Keep me company in my long nights.
The howling and frightful banging,
Turbines whirring, grinding,
Hail peppering windows, roofs, cars,
Followed by a soothing autumn snow
Helping to drown out dreadful noises
Feeding wild nightmares in my heated brain.
Locked in by fear, I stand soulful guard
At cloudy windows, staring at bland walls,
Feeling my cheeks and nose grow colder
As if blood has rushed to my aching feet.
Why does the noontime sun not melt snow?
Or thaw ice on the frozen pond of my life?

FESTIVAL

Big sky naked, no clouds;
People stand in tree shade,
Sun too strong and bold.
People eat meat on sticks,
Others noodles under umbrellas.
People shaped like potatoes
Ignore old people waiting for a chair
Or a slice of small shade.
But potato people do not care:
Eat meat too fast, talk too strong,
Keeping food in mouth short time;
Not taste food like they love it,
Too hurried to enjoy taste on tongue;
Care only about those in tribe with them.

BLOOD OF KIN

Blood is thick when it comes to kin,
Though one day a kin bond must end,
As a brother's damaged heart foretells,
And death knocks finally on his door.

With a sibling's death, reflection unfolds,
Bringing one face-to-face with fate,
Crying seems not to soften the blow,
Oh, for he is gone, but you—remain.

LET ME BE PLAIN

Allow me to smooth my words,
Make them plain as paper,
On which I write words seeded
In soil both fallowed and frozen.

Come a warming sun free from clouds,
And these seedlings will sprout,
Bolder, stronger than daisies in fields.
Now that she whom I love is gone;

She who worked our garden long,
Writing this while caring not
What my ears hear, my eyes feel,
I will see truth in a beauty's death.

I will not mourn my loss,
Though long-suffering pain bleeds,
For death does not hold me close,
As I will not turn my back on fate.

GOODBYE OCTOBER

Mellow October harbinger of winter,

And of mild evenings on a white porch,

Cool mornings, warm bed, cooked eggs.

Dried leaves on a wet wood deck;

Birds flying south suddenly drop in;

Sky blue turns dark grey, clouds mourn.

Mellow October soon gone

As the sun retreats south,

And cold air rises from hardwood floors.

Time comes to reach for warm clothes.

Cut wood, stacked high, for winter fires;

Wake up a furnace from its longish sleep.

I DID NOT WANT THIS FACE

I now look like my father dead:
His jowls, nose and deep-rutted face;
His love of tease, words that cut;

Equally faithless and hot tempered,
But soft at heart when without drink.
Inherited I his blueness and loneliness;

His repressed anger and bitterness deep.
When I shave, I see the resemblance best
In the mirror that has lied not.

It's all there: ailments, eternal flaws, more.
I did not want that face, but had no say on it.
And, yet, on this earthly stage I am terribly him.

THE END